PRO WRESTLING LEGENDS

Steve Austin
The Story of the Wrestler They Call "Stone Cold"

Bill Goldberg

Bret Hart
The Story of the Wrestler They Call "The Hitman"

The Story of the Wrestler
They Call "Hollywood" Hulk Hogan

Randy Savage
The Story of the Wrestler They Call "Macho Man"

The Story of the Wrestler They Call "Sting"

The Story of the Wrestler They Call "The Undertaker"

Jesse Ventura
The Story of the Wrestler They Call "The Body"

CHELSEA HOUSE PUBLISHERS

Steve Austin
The Story of the Wrestler
They Call "Stone Cold"

Dan Ross

Chelsea House Publishers
Philadelphia

Produced by Choptank Syndicate, Inc.

Editor and Picture Researcher: Mary Hull
Design and Production: Lisa Hochstein

CHELSEA HOUSE PUBLISHERS

Editor in Chief: Stephen Reginald
Managing Editor: James D. Gallagher
Production Manager: Pamela Loos
Art Director: Sara Davis
Director of Photography: Judy L. Hasday
Senior Production Editor: LeeAnne Gelletly
Cover Illustrator: Keith Trego

Cover Photos: Sports Action
              Jeff Eisenberg Sports Photography

The Chelsea House World Wide Web site
address is http://www.chelseahouse.com

3 5 7 9 8 6 4 2

Library of Congress Cataloging-in-Publication Data

Ross, Dan.
    Steve Austin : the story of the wrestler they call "Stone Cold" / Dan
      Ross.
           p. cm. — (Pro wrestling legends)
    Includes bibliographical references (p.   ) and index.
       Summary: A biography of the professional wrestler known as
  "Stone Cold" Steve Austin.
       ISBN 0-7910-5403-9   — ISBN 0-7910-5549-3 (pbk.)
       1. Austin, Steve, 1964-   Juvenile literature. 2. Wrestlers —
  United States — Biography — Juvenile literature. [1. Austin, Steve,
  1964- . 2. Wrestlers.] I. Title. II Series.
  GV1196.A97R67 1999
  796.812'092—dc21
  [B]   99-38099
                                                       CIP

Contents

CHAPTER 1
THE DAY OF DESTINY   7

CHAPTER 2
SCHOOL OF HARD KNOCKS   15

CHAPTER 3
THE HOLLYWOOD BLONDS   21

CHAPTER 4
JUST ANOTHER DEAD-END JOB   29

CHAPTER 5
KING OF THE RING   37

CHAPTER 6
THE ROYAL TREATMENT   47

Chronology   61

Further Reading   62

Index   63

1 THE DAY OF DESTINY

Steve Austin had always known this night would arrive. Back in the days when he worked on a loading dock, when he took home just enough money to pay the rent, Austin kept telling himself there was greatness in his future. It was an idea that kept him going.

"Greatness in my future." It was a thought that stuck in his head in 1995, when World Championship Wrestling (WCW) decided he didn't have what it took to be a star. It was a thought that stuck in his head in 1996, when his career hit rock bottom. It was a thought that stuck in his head in 1997, when Owen Hart nearly paralyzed him with a piledriver.

It stuck there. Because deep down, he believed.

On the bleakest days, Austin would stare at himself in the mirror at home or in the locker room. "You don't need anybody," he'd tell the person looking back. "You can do this on your own."

So as "Stone Cold" Steve Austin stepped out of the locker room and began to make his way toward the ring at the Fleet Center in Boston on March 29, 1998, he believed. He had no doubt that his night of greatness had arrived. On this night, he knew he would win the World Wrestling Federation (WWF) World heavyweight championship.

Steve Austin faced severe opposition when he tried to wrestle the WWF World heavyweight championship away from Shawn Michaels at Wrestlemania XIV in Boston, March 29, 1998, but he never doubted that he could win.

WWF officials ordered Hunter Hearst Helmsley and Chyna of DeGeneration X back to the dressing room after they showed up at ringside, trying to interfere on Michaels's behalf during his match with Austin at Wrestlemania XIV.

The only problem was, three men were conspiring to make sure it didn't happen. One man, of course, was Shawn Michaels, the defending champion. Michaels had won the belt from Bret Hart four months earlier and was widely considered the best all-around wrestler in the world. Austin had lost to Michaels several times during the past two years, and for many who closely follow the sport, there was no reason to think Stone Cold would do any better this time.

Another man was Mike Tyson, the former boxing heavyweight champion. Tyson, a fearsome man of enormous strength, had been enlisted by the WWF to serve as special enforcer for the bout. But just a few weeks after that announcement, Tyson joined DeGeneration X, the obnoxious clique of wrestlers led by Michaels. The odds appeared obvious: Austin would be fighting two men instead of one.

Finally, there was Vince McMahon Jr., the owner of the WWF. The relationship between McMahon and Austin had always been less than cordial, and McMahon had publicly said several times that Austin did not fit his ideal of a champion.

Nonetheless, on March 29, 1998, Austin was on the verge of wrestling immortality. His stage was WrestleMania—the event that is to wrestling what the Super Bowl is to football, the World Series is to baseball, or the Indianapolis 500 is to auto racing.

The Fleet Center in Boston was packed with 19,020 fans for WrestleMania XIV. Millions more were watching across the country and around the world on pay-per-view television. The world was waiting.

Austin stared in the dressing room mirror one final time, and decided the face looking back was that of a champion. Then he pulled on his wrestling boots and headed out to the ring. Wearing simple black wrestling trunks and wristbands on both arms, he started the long walk down the runway. The sellout crowd roared with excitement when it spotted the 6' 2", 241-pound muscular bald man with the light brown goatee.

It was time for the main event.

Austin looked straight ahead and ignored the commotion. He had decided to remain true to his nickname, Stone Cold. He would be as cold as ice; focused on the job that had to be done.

Fierce. Unstoppable. Cool. Determined.

Austin spotted Tyson wearing a DeGeneration X T-shirt, and reminded himself that there would be no excuses for failure. He knew that he would have to win this on his own, even if it meant beating the WWF World champion and the former world boxing heavyweight champion.

Michaels arrived in the ring, cocky and confident as always, and perhaps a little more so, considering that Tyson was clearly showing favoritism towards Michaels even before the match started. The ring announcer introduced the wrestlers, and a moment later the bell rang.

Austin wasted no time going after the World champion. With only five minutes gone in the match, Austin had Michaels on the run and a powerful atomic drop by Austin sent the "Heartbreak Kid" thundering to the mat. Austin tried for the quick pin, but the referee only got to two on the three-count before Michaels kicked out.

The intensity increased as the match wore on. Austin retained control of the match with a waistlock that dropped Michaels onto the top rope, then stunned Michaels with a barrage of punches and kicks that sent him sprawling to the arena floor. Austin followed him outside the ring. Michaels was defenseless as Stone Cold threw him facefirst into a television monitor.

Austin continued his relentless assault by slamming Michaels's face into the steel steps, then tossing the champion back into the ring, where two more pin attempts each fell a second short.

Neither of these finely conditioned athletes showed signs of tiring as the match wore on. Sweat poured down both of their faces, but they moved nimbly, quickly, and with remarkable precision. Austin's expression never changed. With 17 minutes expired, he landed a series of right hands and catapulted Michaels into the turnbuckle. He attempted a pin, but got only a two-count.

Austin must have joined many of those in attendance and those viewing at home in wondering: "Isn't there any way of beating this man?"

Michaels recovered and fought back. He gained the advantage, then clamped Austin in a sleeperhold, one of the most dangerous holds in

Boxer Mike Tyson grabs onto Stone Cold's shorts and prepares to throw him back into the ring to battle Shawn Michaels for the WWF Championship at Wrestlemania XIV held on March 29, 1998.

Steve Austin clinches Michaels in a Stone Cold stunner while special enforcer Mike Tyson makes the three-count. A sellout crowd was watching at Fleet Center in Boston when "Stone Cold" Steve Austin became the new WWF World heavyweight champion at Wrestlemania XIV in 1998.

wrestling. When applied properly, the sleeper-hold restricts the flow of blood to the brain and causes the victim to pass out. Austin knew he had little time to break free. Summoning all of his energy, he backed Michaels into the ropes, but the referee got caught between the two wrestlers and was knocked unconscious.

Now Austin knew he was in trouble. Earlier in the match, the referee had evicted Chyna and Hunter Hearst Helmsley, two DeGeneration X members who had come to ringside intending to help Michaels. With the referee knocked out cold, it seemed certain Tyson would take control of the match, and equally certain that Austin would be defeated once again.

Austin had no choice but to fight on. He lifted Michaels by the waist and slammed him into the corner turnbuckle, then connected with a series of punishing forearm blows. Austin again sent Michaels flying into the turnbuckle, then followed up a kick to the midsection with a perfectly-executed backdrop.

The referee was still unconscious. Tyson was still standing, watching outside the ring. Michaels got back to his feet and measured Austin for one of his signature moves: "sweet chin music," a high kick aimed at Austin's chin. But Austin saw it coming. He caught Michaels by the boot, twisted him around, and reversed the maneuver into a Stone Cold stunner, his favorite finishing move.

The moment of truth had arrived. If Austin covered Michaels for the pin, would anyone make the count?

Austin had to try. He hooked Michaels's left leg with his right arm, then forced the champion's shoulders into the mat. He didn't even see what happened next: Tyson bounded into the ring, slid to the mat, and made the count.

One! Two! Three!

Austin was the WWF World champion!

Michaels couldn't believe what had happened! "Iron" Mike Tyson had defied him!

Vince McMahon, watching nearby, contemplated the reality of Austin as champion and was visibly displeased.

And Tyson? Well, he laid out Michaels with a short right jab, then draped a T-shirt with the words *Austin 3:16* over the Heartbreak Kid's fallen body.

Austin held the belt high in the air, soaked in the cheers, and allowed the reality of the situation to sink in. All the years . . . all the hard work . . . and now this, the most improbable ending of all. What an amazing road he'd traveled to get to this amazing moment.

SCHOOL OF
HARD KNOCKS

2

Steve Austin is an extraordinary man who had an ordinary upbringing. Nothing happened in the early years of his life to suggest he would one day become a wrestling champion, much less an icon for the sport during the closing years of the 1990s.

But Austin's success in wrestling is proof that good things can happen to just about anyone. All it takes is luck, skill, and hard work.

"Stone Cold" Steve Austin was born Steve Anderson on December 18, 1964, in Austin, Texas. His biological father disappeared before Steve was old enough to know him, so Steve was raised by his mother, a telephone operator, and her new husband, an insurance salesman.

"We were pretty . . . ordinary kids," Austin told *Rolling Stone* magazine in a 1998 interview. "We just ran around on the street, went to school, did normal stuff. Got in our share of trouble. Typical South Texas stuff."

As far as Steve was concerned, his stepfather was his father, and he took his stepfather's last name, Williams. To this day, when he's not wrestling, Steve goes by the name Williams.

Steve developed an interest in pro wrestling at an early age. He was in fifth grade when he started watching the local

---

Though he acts Stone Cold today, staff at Edna High School in Austin, Texas, remember Steve Williams as a real sweet boy who played football and was a member of the National Honor Society.

wrestling matches on TV. What attracted him the most was the clear distinction between the good guys and the bad guys, the unwavering sportsmanship of the fan favorites and the outright badness of the hated rulebreakers. Ironically, when Steve became a star in the WWF, he would help blur that distinction.

Steve attended Austin's Edna High, where he was voted "Class Favorite" three years out of four. In his senior year, he was voted "Mr. Cowboy of 1983," Edna High's equivalent of homecoming king. A solid athlete, he threw the discus and played football. His high school football coach remembers him as a clean-cut kid with good manners—in other words, the exact opposite of what he would later become in the WWF.

By the time Steve was 18, he had the size— 6' 2" and 241 pounds—to play big-time college football. He attended the University of North Texas and played defensive end.

Unfortunately for Steve, he never graduated from college and wasn't quite good enough to make it into professional football. By 1989, Steve's college scholarship had run out, and he was working 40 hours a week loading and unloading trucks. Working at the loading docks was his only way to make money.

Steve, however, was good at just about everything he put his mind to, and his supervisors on the loading dock appreciated his hard work. They wanted him to train to be a regional manager.

At the time, Steve had been indulging his ongoing love of the mat sport by attending the matches at the Sportatorium in Dallas to watch the Von Erichs wrestle. The Von Erichs were the first family of Texas wrestling, a contingent of staggeringly popular fan favorites whose collective fate would be horrible tragedy. (Four of the five wrestling Von Erich brothers—David, Kerry, Mike, and Chris—died between 1984 and 1993, three of them by committing suicide.)

At the Sportatorium bouts, Steve began to dream about a career in the ring. A career on the loading docks, or even as a regional manager, didn't sound so glamorous in comparison. One day after work, Steve saw an ad for a wrestling school run by wrestler Chris Adams. He decided to take a chance. Five months later, he was the highly touted first graduate of Adams's school.

After graduating from Edna High, Steve attended the University of North Texas on a scholarship and played defensive end for UNT's football team. But when he saw Kerry Von Erich (above) and his brothers compete at the Sportatorium in Dallas, Steve dreamed of a career in wrestling and decided to enroll in wrestling school.

Steve made his pro debut at the Sportatorium in late 1989 and defeated a relatively unknown wrestler named Frogman Leblanc. Things didn't go so well after that.

He lost most of his matches to insignificant stars such as Sheik Braddock and the Punisher, two wrestlers who have long since been forgotten. Later that year, the United States Wrestling Alliance (USWA), which ran divisions in Texas and the southeast United States, transferred him to Tennessee. Steve had been wrestling as Steve Williams, but there was already a famous wrestler by that name: Steve "Dr. Death" Williams. To avoid confusion with the better-known grappler, Steve reluctantly changed his last name to Austin—after his birthplace—because he couldn't think of anything else.

Before long, Steve realized that working in the ring could be no more glamorous than working on the loading docks. The money was terrible, as little as $20 a match, and he often had to drive nearly 500 miles a day from Nashville, Tennessee, to Memphis. He lost most of his matches. There was little to distinguish him from other wrestlers. He had long blond hair and no beard or mustache, and he wore spandex tights. His nickname was simple: "Stunning." His ring performance was anything but.

Steve's career started taking a turn for the better on February 23, 1990, in Dallas, when he met his teacher, Chris Adams, in what was billed as a scientific wrestling match. A scientific wrestler uses the more artistic, amateur wresting moves, as opposed to the showy kicking and punching style of most pro wrestlers. Going into the match, there didn't seem to be any hard feelings between teacher and student, until Austin spit in Adams's face. Adams punched Austin and was disqualified. Two weeks later, again in Dallas, Austin and Jeff Gaylord defeated Adams and Matt Borne in a tag team match at the Sportatorium.

Before long, Austin made his plan clear: he wanted to prove he was a better wrestler than his trainer. In a devious plan that bordered on downright cruelty, Steve recruited Jeannie Clark, Adams's ex-wife, as his valet.

The Austin-Clark tandem quickly became the most hated duo in Texas. Every Friday night at the Sportatorium, they'd attack and brutally double-team Adams. Adams's wife, Toni, was drawn into the fray. In singles matches between Austin and Adams, USWA officials were so concerned about the women interfering that they threatened $10,000 fines if either interfered. Jeannie and Toni interfered anyway. On July 4, 1990, Austin piledrived Adams outside of the ring; at the same time inside the ring, Toni choked Jeannie to near-unconsciousness.

Although the feud was never settled, Austin held his own against the 13-year veteran, displaying keen mat and aerial skills, and a killer instinct. Steve was voted Rookie of the Year for 1990 by the readers of *Pro Wrestling Illustrated* magazine.

He also got the attention of WCW, which signed him to a contract that paid $75,000 a year. In only about 12 months, Steve had come a long way from making $20 a night. He was on the verge of stardom.

Whatever happened to Adams's ex-wife Jeannie Clark? She followed Austin to WCW. Before long, she would become Jeannie Austin, Steve's wife.

THE HOLLYWOOD BLONDS

3

Steve Austin made his WCW debut on May 31, 1991, in Houston, Texas, where he defeated Sam Houston. Four days later in Birmingham, Alabama, he beat Bobby Eaton, a former tag team standout, for the WCW TV title. As debut weeks go, the only way Austin could have made a bigger splash was if he had won the WCW World or U.S. title. The title victory marked him for greatness.

TV championships are the most volatile belts in wrestling. Champions are forced to defend their titles far more often than other titleholders. Because title shots are more plentiful, there are many more contenders for the belt. Eaton, whom Austin had beaten for the TV belt, had been champion for only 25 days. Arn Anderson, the champion before Eaton, had held the belt for a little over three months. Austin was the fourth man in 1991 to hold the TV title.

He was also the last. Over the course of two TV title reigns, Austin would wear the belt for 429 of the next 455 days, and turn back challenges from such top-notch competitors as Johnny B. Badd, Dustin Rhodes, Scott Steiner, and Brian Pillman. The first of his TV title reigns, lasting 10 months, would fall just eight days short of matching the longest WCW TV title reign of all time: 337 days by Arn Anderson.

When Steve Austin made his pro wrestling debut, WCW warned him that a no-nonsense wrestler in black shorts was not very marketable. Nevertheless, Austin decided to keep his image.

The greatest television wrestler of all time, Arn Anderson holds the record for the longest WCW TV title reign in history, with 337 days. Steve Austin fell just eight days short of matching Anderson's record in 1991.

Austin had a right to be cocky. When he declared himself "the world's greatest athlete," it was difficult to argue that he wasn't, even if he had never held the WCW World title.

"Mike Tyson was the world's greatest boxer long before he won the heavyweight title in that sport," Austin declared. "Pacing and seasoning are important in wrestling, as they are in any sport. I will decide when the time is right to win the World title."

Austin's arrogance and confidence about his good looks quickly turned him into one of the most hated men in WCW.

In October of 1991, manager Paul E. Dangerously, who had a reputation for managing ruthless rulebreakers, returned to WCW. Dangerously vowed to destroy the federation "piece by piece" by putting together the most destructive organization in the sport: the Dangerous Alliance. Austin joined Dangerously's group, standing alongside Arn Anderson, Rick Rude, Larry Zbyszko, and Bobby Eaton.

Dangerously constantly interfered on Austin's behalf, and members of the Dangerous Alliance, including Austin, frequently interfered in their enemies' matches. Austin's first TV title reign ended on April 27, 1992, with a loss to Barry Windham. His second TV title reign started on May 23, 1992, when he regained the belt from Windham in Atlanta.

Dangerously's interference had become so problematic that WCW officials ordered him to be suspended in a cage above the ring for Austin's TV title defense against Rick Steamboat at Clash of the Champions XX.

Steamboat was a former WCW World champion and one of the finest scientific wrestlers in history. He won the match—and ended Austin's second TV title reign—by crawling under the ring, emerging at the opposite side, mounting the top rope, and executing a marvelous flying bodypress.

"I didn't realize what a sneak Ricky Steamboat is," Austin complained. "Crawling under the ring and attacking me from the top rope? Go back and watch the tape. If he faces me head-on at that point in the match, he's pinned, plain and simple."

Austin hardly had a right to complain about Steamboat's chicanery. After all, countless times Dangerously had interfered on his behalf.

To Austin's credit, he didn't spend much time pouting. A few months after the loss, Austin began teaming with "Flyin'" Brian Pillman, an outstanding aerial wrestler. Pillman, like Austin, had blond hair, although his was long, down to his back, while Austin's was now cropped close. Like Austin, Pillman was an outstanding all-around wrestler. The duo called themselves "the Hollywood Blonds." Their target was Steamboat and Shane Douglas, the WCW World tag team champions.

By no means were the Hollywood Blonds a conventional tag team. They often argued during matches and nearly came to blows on several occasions. They would stop in the middle of a match and mock a fallen opponent. One of their weirdest gimmicks was making believe they were filming their opponents, like Hollywood cameramen. Cocky and obnoxious, the Blonds were hateable, compelling, and one of the most talented tag teams ever formed. They blended brawling and science into a lethal combination.

"Illegal doesn't mean you can't do it, it means you can't get caught doing it," Pillman said. "Fan favorites wrestle under some invisible, outdated code. You know what? It doesn't mean squat unless you have the belt around your waist."

Through all the arguing and disagreements, a strong dedication to winning the World tag team title kept them together. On March 2, 1993, Austin and Pillman faced Steamboat and Douglas in a World tag team title match in Macon, Georgia. Pillman and Steamboat were the legal men in the ring, but Pillman was dazed and Steamboat had the upper hand. Referee Randy Anderson, however, had his back turned, and was arguing with Douglas. Taking advantage of the situation, Austin grabbed one of the championship belts and used it to knock out Steamboat. Then Austin rolled Pillman on top of Steamboat and made the pin before Anderson turned around.

Steamboat complained, but Austin denied any wrongdoing. WCW officials upheld the decision.

The Blonds became a dominating duo, beating team after team, by any means necessary. Nine days before they were scheduled to defend the belts against Arn Anderson and Paul Roma at Clash of the Champions XXIV on August 18, the Blonds stepped into the ring in Atlanta for what they thought would be an easy match against Mark Starr and Frankie Lancaster.

During the match Pillman suffered a broken right ankle, which sidelined him for two months. "Lord" Steven Regal substituted for Pillman at Clash of the Champions, but Anderson and Roma won the belts when Anderson pinned Austin.

Partnerless, Austin returned to singles wrestling. Without asking Pillman's opinion, Austin hired Colonel Robert Parker as his manager.

Pillman was enraged. He didn't want Parker managing the Hollywood Blonds. When Pillman attacked Parker at a TV taping, Austin sided with his new manager and turned against Pillman. The Blonds were through.

Steve managed to keep an eye on his goal of winning another major singles title. He got his chance at the Starrcade '93 pay-per-view on December 27 in a match against WCW U.S.

In 1992 Steve Austin teamed with aerial wrestler Flyin' Brian Pillman (left) to create the Hollywood Blonds, a short-lived WCW tag team known for its unconventional behavior.

Shortly after his debut, wrestling broadcasters started comparing Steve Austin to Ric Flair (right) who, as a young wrestler, had exuded the same in-your-face confidence and poise as Austin.

champion Dustin Rhodes. Austin beat Rhodes in a controversial best-of-three-falls match and won the title.

Steve's career prospects were rising rapidly. His salary had doubled to $156,000 a year. He was a recognized star who had proven himself in both tag team and singles competition. He was despised by the fans, which was a good thing: in wrestling, the worst thing of all is to go unnoticed.

Austin's U.S. title reign was impressive. He defeated the Great Muta and Johnny B. Badd, and he feuded with Pillman. Eventually, Austin dumped Parker as his manager, but his title reign continued until Clash of the Champions XXVII on August 24, 1994, when he lost to Steamboat. Austin had been exercising dubious means to retain the title, like getting himself disqualified on purpose. WCW Commissioner Nick Bockwinkel informed Austin that if he got himself disqualified, Steamboat would be awarded the belt.

The stipulation wasn't necessary. When Austin tossed Steamboat over the top rope, Steamboat held on to the ropes and flung himself back inside the ring. He then pinned a stunned Austin for the belt.

Although Austin couldn't have known it at the time, that loss to Steamboat was the beginning of his end in WCW. He and Steamboat were scheduled to wrestle at the Fall Brawl '94 pay-per-view, but Steamboat had to back out due to an injury. Immediately, Bockwinkel declared Hacksaw Duggan as Austin's substitute opponent. Duggan needed only 27 seconds to pin Austin.

"I can't believe this! This is bogus!" Austin shouted. "Bockwinkel should be fired! How can he make a decision like this?!"

Well, as events transpired, Bockwinkel wasn't the one who got fired.

Austin was.

JUST ANOTHER DEAD-END JOB

The wrestling world was in the midst of an upheaval when Austin lost the WCW U.S. title to Hacksaw Duggan. Since 1984, Vince McMahon's WWF had dominated the sport in terms of attendance, television ratings, and overall popularity. The WWF had all of the big stars, and its annual WrestleMania pay-per-view was considered the Super Bowl of wrestling.

The WWF's rise to power had coincided with the arrival of Hulk Hogan, who quickly won the World heavyweight title in 1984 and became the greatest superstar in wrestling history. As far as many Americans were concerned, the WWF was the major league of wrestling because of Hogan, whose appeals to children to say their prayers and take their vitamins won over millions of fans. WCW was overmatched.

All that changed in 1994. Ted Turner, the billionaire cable TV magnate who owned WCW, finally decided to use his vast wealth to compete with the WWF on more even terms. Turner proved to be a formidable foe for McMahon. In June, he pulled off a remarkable coup by luring Hogan from the WWF. With that one signing, WCW had taken a major step toward becoming the preeminent wrestling federation in the world.

Steve Austin struggled to find a new image and name after losing his job with the WCW and then joining the ranks of the WWF.

Austin lost his chance to regain the WCW title when his injured opponent Steamboat was replaced with former WWF star Hacksaw Duggan (right). It took Duggan just 27 seconds to pin Austin at the Fall Brawl in 1994. Duggan and other former WWF wrestlers like Hulk Hogan, Brutus Beefcake, and Randy Savage, were lured away from the WWF to help boost WCW's television ratings.

Turner didn't stop there. He also signed Brutus "the Barber" Beefcake and Hacksaw Duggan, and in December he pulled off another coup by stealing former World champion Randy Savage from the WWF. The WWF and WCW were at war, and WCW was winning.

Austin was both a victim and a victor in this war.

Many insiders believed that Duggan received the impromptu shot at Austin because he was

Hogan's friend, and WCW wanted to keep Hogan happy. WCW officials never commented on that allegation and it was never proven.

Whatever the story, Austin was definitely losing his marketability. WCW promoters had long ago told Austin that a scientific wrestler who wore black trunks and black boots wasn't very marketable, and the events of 1994 only served to prove their point. With Hogan and Savage in the federation, WCW fans no longer cared about Austin. The only matches they wanted to see were Hogan or Savage against Ric Flair for the World title. Nothing else mattered.

In the fall of 1994, Austin found himself in a horrible position. He was a former WCW U.S., TV, and World tag team champion without much hope of ever winning the World title he so coveted—the title he claimed he'd win whenever he felt like winning it. Little by little, Austin had become a forgotten man.

"Steve Austin was good, but he was never as good as he thought he was," said Rick Rude, a former teammate in the Dangerous Alliance. "The guy believed more in his press clippings than in himself. The Steve Austin phenomenon was created by writers and broadcasters, not by anything he ever did in the ring."

Austin did nothing to help his cause. Duggan won a rematch at the Halloween Havoc '94 pay-per-view when Austin was disqualified for tossing him over the top rope. Austin hired former World champion Harley Race as his manager, his third manager in a year, hoping Race would enable him to focus on beating Duggan. Nothing worked. In a rematch against Duggan, Austin tore ligaments in his left knee.

He was expected to be out of action for nearly a year, but he returned after only three months.

Austin returned to an even bleaker situation. During the summer of 1995, he went to Japan to wrestle. On his third night there, Austin failed to connect on a maneuver from the top turnbuckle when his opponent moved out of the way. As he landed, he felt a tear in his right arm. Although in pain, Austin wrestled until the end of his Japanese tour, but when he got back to America, he found out his tricep had become detached and he would need an operation.

Austin didn't receive much sympathy from WCW officials, who seized the opportunity to dump a wrestler they no longer wanted. As Austin told *Rolling Stone* magazine, WCW president Eric Bischoff called him one day and said, "I'm not going to sugarcoat anything, Steve. I'm going to tell you like it is. Based on the money we're paying you and the amount of days you've been incapacitated, we're going to exercise our right to terminate the agreement." In other words, Austin had been fired.

Austin was 30 years old, injured, jobless, and extremely bitter, especially toward Hogan, whom he felt had been catered to by WCW. "What good is it to . . . make a name and reputation for yourself, and become totally forgotten when the fair-haired boy shows up?" Austin told *Pro Wrestling Illustrated* magazine. "Who needs that? The fact is that I have been competing with a knee injury that would confine most people to a bed. I also hurt my left arm a couple of months ago. That basically made me a one-armed wrestler. But even with one arm, I'm still better than 90 percent of the wrestlers

Hulk Hogan's switch to WCW coincided with a downhill slide in Austin's WCW career. The Hulkster dominated the attention of WCW fans when he joined the federation in 1994, and Austin's popularity declined. Unwilling to carry a wrestler who couldn't command huge crowds, WCW president Eric Bischoff terminated Austin's contract.

out there. But WCW didn't want to hear about that."

A few years later, in an interview on the cable network TSN's *Off the Record* program, Austin expressed his anger at Bischoff for not firing him in person.

"I lived 30 miles down from the CNN Center at the time," Austin said. All he had to do was say, 'Come down to the office. We need to talk.' I just got pissed off [that] they fired me over the phone. That's a pretty lame thing to do to a person who works for you for four years."

Austin quickly found work. He was signed by Extreme Championship Wrestling (ECW), the small Pennsylvania-based federation that had a reputation for extreme violence and extremely bizarre behavior by its wrestlers. For Austin, this was clearly a backward career step. The only way of moving forward would have been to sign with the WWF, but, as he told *Rolling Stone*, he was too proud to pick up the phone and make the call.

In ECW, Austin feuded with the Sandman, an offbeat character who chain-smoked and drank beer in the ring. They were scheduled to meet at ECW's November to Remember card on November 18, 1995, but Austin put Sandman out of commission with a pre-match attack. He ended up wrestling, and losing to, the 5' 7", 187-pound Mikey Whipwreck.

Being in ECW gave Austin an outlet to vent his anger at WCW. In his interviews, he mocked Eric Bischoff and Hulk Hogan. He told the world how WCW had turned his back on him when he was injured. And he waited for the WWF to come calling.

Less than a month after Austin had made his ECW debut, the WWF did call. The federation signed him to a contract and brought him in as "the Ringmaster" under the guidance of Ted DiBiase, who was known as the "Million-Dollar Man"

DiBiase, a fine scientific wrestler, taught Austin his "Million-Dollar Dream" finisher, the move which would come to be known as the "Stone Cold stunner." In the move, Austin would stand in front of his opponent, reach an arm around his opponent's neck, then drop to the mat, taking his opponent with him head-first to the canvas. The move was extremely effective. Austin went undefeated in his first three months in the WWF, but his Ringmaster gimmick wasn't going over well with WWF fans, who simply ignored him.

The Ringmaster was a dud. Austin knew that. He shaved his head and left his goatee, but nobody cared. He talked and talked in interviews, but nobody listened. He knew he had to do something to change his image for the better, and he liked the idea of transforming himself into a cold-blooded rulebreaker who didn't care about anybody but himself. WWF promoters also liked the idea but couldn't decide upon an appropriate nickname.

Then, one day, Austin and his wife, Jeannie, were sitting around their house in Georgia, bemoaning the fact that he couldn't get his big break. She made him a cup of hot tea. He sat there and moped. "Just drink your tea before it gets stone cold," she chided.

Both their heads popped up at the same time.

"Stone Cold" Steve Austin was born. One of the first losers in WCW's war against the WWF was about to become the biggest winner of all.

5 KING OF THE RING

The WWF had fallen on hard times by the middle of 1996. Several more of its stars had defected to WCW, including former World champion Kevin Nash and former Inter-continental champion Scott Hall. Suddenly, *Monday Nitro*, WCW's live weekly TV showcase, was attracting more viewers than the WWF's *Monday Night Raw*.

The WWF desperately needed a hero, a high-profile star, but where could it turn? The most likely candidates—Hulk Hogan, Randy Savage, Lex Luger, Ric Flair, Nash, and Hall—were all on the other side. As WCW prospered, the WWF slumped.

Austin seemed an unlikely prospect to save the federation. After losing to Savio Vega at the In Your House pay-per-view on May 26, 1996, Austin also lost the services of his manager. DiBiase had vowed to leave the WWF if Austin lost, and he made good on his promise.

Austin's plan was to follow through on the promise he had made to himself: not only to be nicknamed Stone Cold, but to develop a stone-cold attitude. He wanted to be known as a ruthless, arrogant rulebreaker who would stop at nothing to win a match and didn't care what anybody thought about him. When he talked, he made sure people listened, and when other people talked, he made sure he turned his back.

When Stone Cold got tired of listening to Jake "the Snake" Roberts quote chapter and verse, he defeated him at the June 23, 1996, King of the Ring tournament and declared that his victory be known as "Austin 3:16."

His first most important night in the WWF came at the 1996 King of the Ring tournament on June 23. In the semifinals, Austin pinned Marc Mero. In the finals, Austin defeated Jake "the Snake" Roberts, who had been injured earlier in the evening, by using a neckbreaker to get the pin in less than five minutes.

"Steve Austin's time has come," he vowed. "You're looking at the next WWF champion."

Austin's arrogance emerged over the next few months. He was selective about whom he wrestled, refusing to step into the ring against anyone he felt wasn't good enough. He backed up his arrogance at SummerSlam '96 by taking merely one minute and 51 seconds to pin former

When Scott Hall, aka Razor Ramon, and Kevin Nash, aka Diesel, defected from the WWF and stormed the halls of WCW, they helped boost the ratings for WCW's live weekly program, Monday Nitro.

World champion Yokozuna, a 589-pound Sumo wrestler whom others had failed to budge.

The Stone Cold stunner was a brutally effective finishing maneuver. Austin used it against Hunter Hearst Helmsley, Savio Vega, and Marc Mero. He promised to use it against former World champion Bret Hart at the 1996 Survivor Series, but Hart survived two stunners and won by pinfall.

Meanwhile, the oddest thing was happening. Instead of booing Austin, as fans of the past would have done, many fans were cheering him. For some reason, the antihero was becoming the hero. Despite being neither polite nor politically correct, refusing to say the right thing or kiss up to anyone, and saying annoying and often vulgar things in his TV interviews, Austin was becoming a star—not necessarily for what he did in the ring, but for what he said.

Indeed, the line between rulebreaker and fan favorite had become blurred beyond recognition. The rulebreaker was a fan favorite!

A prime example of this had been Austin's treatment of Roberts after the King of the Ring. Roberts was a Bible-thumping fan favorite with the motto "Jake 3:16." Austin had told him what he thought about Jake 3:16.

"You sit there and you thump your Bible and you say your prayers and it didn't get you anywhere," Austin said. "You talk about your Psalms, you talk about John 3:16. Well, Austin 3:16 says, 'I just whipped your [butt].'"

Within days, fans were bringing their Austin 3:16 banners to WWF cards. Within months, the WWF was sending out shipments of Austin 3:16 T-shirts that were selling faster than any other shirts in the arenas. Many fans even sided with Austin in the feud he started with Bret Hart, who had been one of the most popular wrestlers in the world. Thanks to Austin, the fans would eventually turn against Hart.

Looking back, there's no doubt Austin's feud with Hart changed his career. It gave him the chance to beat a wrestler who not only referred to himself as "the best there is, the best there was, and the best there ever will be," but who had a right to that claim. When Hart, Austin, and Hunter Hearst Helmsley met in a three-way match on January 10, 1997, Hart and Austin were so concerned with making sure each other didn't win that Helmsley won. The day after that, Austin interfered in a Hart vs. Helmsley match, helping Helmsley win.

Austin turned in one of the most remarkable performances in Royal Rumble history when he eliminated 10 other combatants, including Hart, to win the match and earn a shot against World champion Shawn Michaels at WrestleMania XIII. The win, however, was highly controversial. With 50 minutes gone, Hart had dumped Austin over the top rope, apparently eliminating him, but the referees were busy elsewhere. Austin reentered the ring and went on to victory.

WWF president Gorilla Monsoon went to the videotape, saw what happened, and ordered a four-way match involving Austin, Hart, Big Van Vader, and The Undertaker—all former World champions in the WWF and WCW. The winner was originally scheduled to get the World title shot at WrestleMania, but then Michaels surprisingly vacated the title because of a knee injury. Monsoon changed the four-way bout into a title match, which Hart went on to win.

Enraged, Austin went on a rampage in the weeks following the match. He attacked Hart both verbally and physically, with such intensity that people started asking, "Has Steve Austin gone crazy?"

Indeed, WWF announcer Jim Ross asked that very question on *Monday Night Raw.* "'Stone Cold' Steve Austin, what's wrong with you? Have you gone over the edge?"

Replied Austin: "What's wrong with me? I done went over the edge. Gorilla Monsoon makes up a Final Four match where I'm a participant, and that was never supposed to happen. I won the Royal Rumble fair and square by throwing 29 pieces of trash out of the ring. There ain't no such thing as the instant replay rule in the WWF. Shawn Michaels hurts his knee and can't wrestle. By all rights, that championship should be mine. You hold me back, this organization holds me back, because I ain't all glitz and glamour, smiling for the pub- licity shots."

He certainly wasn't. Never had been. Never would be.

"You could laugh if it wasn't so frustrating for Austin," said Brian Pillman, Austin's former teammate. "I've known him a long time, and I can tell just by watching him that he's nearly insane over this. I think the only way you might see him calm down is if he wins the WWF title. Maybe, but I don't know. He's out there, man."

Yeah, he was out there—and getting a lot of attention.

WWF fans were wearing Austin 3:16 T- shirts and mimicking Austin's favorite phrases: "because 'Stone Cold' said so" and "that's the bottom line." Austin never held back. Asked

When Bret Hart wrestled the World heavyweight title out from under Austin's nose in 1997, Austin swore revenge against the entire Hart family. Austin's feud with longtime fan favorite Bret Hart helped establish his reputation as a rulebreaker.

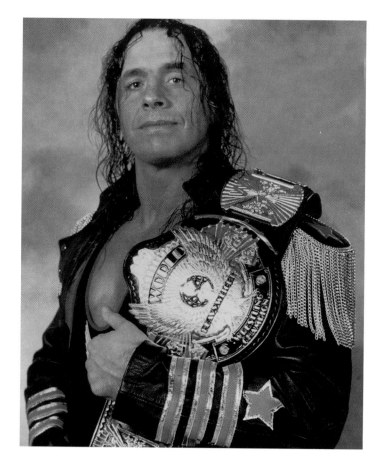

about WWF head Vince McMahon, Austin said, "He's got a big mouth, too big for my tastes, but he's a smart man because he signed me to a contract." Commenting on the Hart family, he said, "The only reason they're still around is because I don't want them to go away yet. I have too much fun kickin' the hell out of all of 'em. Why? Because 'Stone Cold' wants it that way."

Austin was beyond control. He also had some sensational matches, such as his showdown with Hart at WrestleMania XIII. These two outstanding wrestlers put on a show, and

Austin saved his best for a one-minute stretch late in the match. After whipping Hart brutally into the turnbuckle, he kicked him to the ground, then dropped him onto the top rope. Austin grabbed an extension cord and tried to choke Hart, who narrowly escaped with his life. Three minutes later, Hart clamped on his "sharpshooter" leglock finisher. With blood pouring down his face, Austin never submitted—because he passed out from the pain. Wrestler Ken Shamrock, who was the guest referee for the match, called for the bell and awarded the match to Hart, who still refused to break the hold. Austin finally recovered, and it took seven WWF referees to get him back to the dressing room. The match was voted the year's best by the readers of *Pro Wrestling Illustrated* magazine.

Austin went to war with the entire Hart family: Bret, Bret's brother Owen, and Bret's brother-in-law Davey Boy Smith, also known as the Hart Foundation. As the fans turned against Hart, a longtime favorite, they became even more enthusiastic in their appreciation for Austin. When Shawn Michaels saved Austin from an attack by the Hart Foundation, the fans' collective allegiance was settled. They were all for Stone Cold . . . and that was the bottom line.

Wrestling had gone topsy-turvy. Michaels saved Austin not because he liked him, but because he hated the Hart Foundation even more!

Michaels and Austin formed a tag team and went after the Hart Foundation, which held the WWF World tag team belts. On May 26, 1997, Michaels and Austin defeated Owen Hart and

Smith for the belts, but the postmatch celebration was nonexistent; they hated each other too much to celebrate.

Who were the rulebreakers? Who were the fan favorites? Who liked whom? Who hated whom? Whom could anybody trust? The old lines of distinction had been wiped away. On June 8, 1997, Michaels and Austin went one-on-one in a match that ended with both men being disqualified. Since when did championship tag team partners wrestle against each other?

Austin didn't even enjoy the cheers of the fans. Before taking on Bret Hart in Cleveland, Austin snapped, "I ain't trying to beat him for any . . . fans or any American cause. I'll just kick his butt for my own personal enjoyment!"

Yes, the fans cheered that, too!

Despite his rising career prospects, despite the fact that hundreds of thousands of fans were wearing T-shirts bearing his name and likeness, Austin had not achieved any of his WWF goals. A singles heavyweight title had proven elusive.

On August 3, Austin stepped into the ring at SummerSlam '97 and squared off against Intercontinental champion Owen Hart. Beating the younger Hart would be an important stepping-stone for Austin, because it would make him the number one contender for the World title.

Austin had promised to kiss Owen's rear end if he lost the match, and for a while it looked as if that might happen. With 15 minutes gone, Owen gave Austin a piledriver, a move in which a wrestler places his victim's head between his thighs then drops to the mat. When executed properly—or improperly, depending upon your point of view—it can give the victim either a very bad headache or a career-threatening case of paralysis.

"When he landed," Austin recalled, "between his weight and mine, there was close to 500 pounds coming down on the top of my head. He dropped me flat on my head. I laid there in front of 20,000 people not being able to move an arm or a leg."

Austin lost the feeling in his neck and arms. Fear rushed through his mind. "I thought I was a quadriplegic," he would later tell *Rolling Stone* magazine. Finally, after about a minute, Austin was able to wiggle his toes, then his fingers. He rolled over onto his stomach and summoned all of his remaining strength to crawl over to Hart, grab him by the tights, pull him down to the mat, and cover him for the pin.

Remarkably, Austin was the new WWF Intercontinental champion.

But there was no victory party that night. Austin was badly injured. The piledriver had severely damaged his neck. Over the following days, he underwent a battery of tests, including several MRIs. Doctors told him he had suffered acute spinal shock syndrome and had come within a hair's breadth of being paralyzed for life.

Just when he was on the verge of super-stardom, Austin had received the biggest jolt of his life. He didn't know if he would ever wrestle again.

6 THE ROYAL TREATMENT

Steve replayed the videotape of SummerSlam '97 over and over again. He never got used to seeing his head being driven into the canvas with such unimaginable force. The sight of his head glancing off the mat and jamming into his spine made Austin feel sick every time he watched the tape.

"To be specific, Steve had been struck with transient quadriplegia," said Dr. Joseph Torg, an orthopedic surgeon in Philadelphia. "In effect, his spinal cord had been pinched, leaving him temporarily paralyzed. Spinal shock isn't a common occurrence, but when it does happen, it is usually seen on the football field."

At first, Austin hoped he'd need only a few weeks to recover and return to the ring. After consulting with Dr. Torg, however, he realized his return could be much further away. His body had suffered significant damage and a recurrence of the paralysis was possible if Austin suffered another similar blow.

"Unfortunately for Steve, the only precaution he can take is to prevent his head from being rammed into the mat again," Dr. Torg said. "That's why we're reserving judgment on whether it's wise for Steve to continue wrestling."

Because he was worried that his wrestling career might be over, Austin became depressed. He was angry at the WWF and

Steve Austin pushes WWF owner Vince McMahon Jr. into the water during a public appearance. While feuding with McMahon, Austin took every opportunity to humiliate the federation owner.

47

the magazines that seemed to be capitalizing on his misfortune.

Steve was also angry when WWF commissioner Sergeant Slaughter stripped him of the Intercontinental title. He didn't care about the risks involved; he wanted to return to the ring and begged the WWF to grant him clearance. When Vince McMahon suggested he be patient and work within the system, Austin used a Stone Cold stunner on McMahon. The next night, McMahon offered Austin three options: get clearance from doctors, quit the WWF, or sign a waiver absolving the WWF of responsibility if he is injured during a match. After consulting with Dr. Torg, Austin signed the waiver. Suddenly, his attitude brightened.

Owen Hart (right) executed a piledriver on Austin that momentarily paralyzed him during their August 3, 1997, match for the WWF Intercontinental title. Although Austin managed to cover Hart for the pin and win the title, he had suffered acute spinal shock syndrome, a condition that his doctors warned could worsen if he continued to wrestle.

Risking paralysis, if not his life, Austin returned to the ring on October 25, 1997, and used his Stone Cold stunner to defeat Hunter Hearst Helmsley. The next night, he used another stunner to defeat the man known as Triple-H.

The injury had two important effects on Steve's career. To the fans, it made him even more of a hero than before, because he had overcome this horrible injury and shown incredible guts by returning to the ring. To Vince McMahon, it made Austin a man of whom to be wary. After all, how many people have the nerve to physically assault the person who signs their paycheck?

There was one other important order of business. Steve wasn't desperate to step into the ring against Owen Hart, but he knew he had to. He needed to prove to himself and to Hart that he wasn't afraid of him. Something else was on the line at the Survivor Series pay-per-view on November 9, 1997, in Montreal: Hart had won the Intercontinental title in the tournament, filling the vacancy created by Austin's injury.

Austin wrestled a cautious match and was wary of Owen's piledriver. But he wrestled a fine match and used his Stone Cold stunner to become a two-time Intercontinental champion.

The Austin legend was growing by the day. At the DeGeneration X pay-per-view on December 7, he drove his truck to the ring for a match against Rocky Maivia, a member of the DeGeneration X clique of wrestlers. Austin pinned Maivia, then executed his Stone Cold stunner on D-Lo Brown, another DeGeneration X member, on top of the truck!

The next night at WWF's *Monday Night Raw*, McMahon berated Austin for using his truck as a weapon and ordered him to defend the title against Maivia. Austin refused, then walked outside and tossed the belt into an adjacent river. McMahon declared Maivia the new champion.

Once again, Steve had captured the public's imagination. He had effectively said to his boss, "Take this job and shove it." He refused to be pushed around. He refused to follow orders. Austin was living out the dream of every working man. The fans loved it.

Steve showed his disdain for McMahon and the Intercontinental title by not even trying to regain the belt. He had decided the time was right to make a run at the WWF World heavyweight title.

Austin's first order of business was to enter the Royal Rumble and try to win it for the second year in a row. The winner of the match on January 18 would receive a shot at the World championship at WrestleMania XIV. His intensity and aggressiveness increased in the weeks leading up to the Rumble. He used his Stone Cold stunner on a dozen Rumble entrants, fan favorites and rulebreakers alike. Austin showed utter disregard for the distinction that used to exist in wrestling between good and bad—the same distinction that had drawn him to the sport back when he was a teenager. When the bell rang for the Rumble, Austin was ready.

He was the 24th man to enter the ring for the 30-man event, and he was the last man to leave it. He stormed the ring with a vengeance and eventually eliminated Maivia to win the

Determined to wrest the championship belt away from Austin, WWF owner Vince McMahon Jr. repeatedly matched Austin against such giants as Undertaker (right) and Kane.

match and get a shot against World champion Shawn Michaels at WrestleMania.

Mike Tyson, the former heavyweight boxing champion, attended the Royal Rumble in San Jose, California. He sat in a luxury suite and rooted for Austin. The next night at *Monday Night Raw*, McMahon announced that Tyson would be the guest enforcer for the Austin vs. Michaels bout at WrestleMania. This wasn't unusual. In an attempt to attract attention, the WWF had frequently used guest referees and timekeepers for WrestleMania. But when Austin came out and berated Tyson, and Tyson joined Michaels's DeGeneration X, the special enforcer no longer looked unbiased.

Seemingly everyone but the fans was against Austin. A few days before Wrestle-Mania, McMahon declared that Austin as World champion would be "a public relations and promotional nightmare." Certainly, both rule-breakers and fan favorites had held the WWF World title, but Austin was neither. Despite his penchant for beating up referees, using vulgar language, and breaking the rules, he was the most popular wrestler in the federation. Austin was a nonconformist, and McMahon didn't like nonconformists.

McMahon could do nothing but watch and hope that either Michaels would beat Austin fair and square, or that Tyson's biased inter-vention would spell doom for Stone Cold and end his title hopes.

McMahon, along with a sellout crowd in Boston, Massachusetts, watched with great anticipation on March 29, 1998, as Austin stepped into the ring against Michaels. Things looked bad for Austin when Tyson showed up wearing a DX T-shirt, and even worse when DXers Chyna and Helmsley came to the ring to support Michaels.

But when WWF officials ordered Chyna and Helmsley back to the dressing room, Austin launched an amazing attack on Michaels. He scored four two-counts within 90 seconds as Michaels clutched his oft-injured back in pain. Austin was wrestling with a bad leg, but he was resilient as Michaels dominated the middle minutes of the match.

With 16 minutes gone, Michaels applied a figure-four leglock, but Austin reversed it into a figure-four of his own. Then Michaels clamped on a sleeperhold, but Austin backed his foe into the turnbuckle, knocking the referee unconscious.

Austin was in trouble. He was at DX's mercy. He landed a Stone Cold stunner, covered Michaels, and waited—futilely, he thought—for somebody to make the count.

To Michaels's amazement, Tyson bounded into the ring and made the three-count. Austin had won his first WWF World title.

On the surface, McMahon should have been delighted with Austin's victory. After all, Austin was not only extremely popular, he was the most marketable wrestler in the federation. T-shirts bearing his name and likeness were outselling all other wrestling merchandise by a wide margin. Austin, who 10 years earlier was making $20 a night, was suddenly a multi-million-dollar property.

But McMahon wasn't happy with his new champion at all and vowed to mold Austin into an ideal corporate champion. Not surprisingly, Austin resisted being molded into anything he didn't want to be.

"Nobody can stand that piece of trash because he's a liar, a cheat, and even worse, a . . . yella coward," Austin said. "All this garbage started because Vince was trying to load the deck all the time for his so-called superstars, like Bret Hart and Shawn Michaels. He even went so far as to get Mike Tyson to help him. Yeah, Vince knew what he was doin'. It was a conspiracy if I ever saw one, but it ain't gonna work when he's dealin' with Stone Cold."

During their feud, Austin challenged WWF owner Vince McMahon Jr. to tests of strength like this arm wrestling match, which Austin won.

McMahon did everything in his power to change Austin, and Austin did everything in his power to humiliate McMahon. He even challenged McMahon to a match at *Monday Night Raw*. McMahon reluctantly accepted. The fans in Philadelphia that night gleefully chanted, "Vince is dead! Vince is dead!," in anticipation that their new hero would destroy his boss. The match never happened because Dude Love interfered before it got started.

Then McMahon assigned himself as the outside-the-ring referee for the Austin vs. Hunter Hearst Helmsley match at the Skydome in Toronto on May 23. He also made Dude Love the timekeeper. McMahon was doing everything in his power to rob Austin of the belt, but the plan still failed. Despite McMahon's interference, Austin pinned Helmsley, and McMahon threw a tantrum.

McMahon tried again. He officiated a match between Austin and Dude Love and made his close associates, Pat Patterson and Jerry Brisco, the guest ring announcer and guest time-keeper. During the match, McMahon kept changing the rules. The match ended when Austin executed his Stone Cold stunner on Love, then dragged McMahon, unconscious from an earlier blow, over to Love and slapped the mat three times with McMahon's hand.

McMahon was relentless. He sent Dude Love, Helmsley, The Undertaker, and Kane after Austin, but none of them could wrest the belt from Stone Cold. McMahon ordered Austin to defend the title in three-way matches, in which Austin had to fend off two challengers at the same time, but Austin kept finding ways to win.

For the first time in two years, the WWF was winning, too. Thanks to Austin's popularity and the unusual feud between a wrestler and his hated boss, the WWF was back on top in the wrestling business. Its Monday night broadcasts were drawing larger audiences than WCW's *Monday Nitro* for the first time since June 1996. Austin had achieved bonafide superstardom. He was the most recognized name in the sport.

The demands on Austin's time increased. He was a guest on the TV show *Live with Regis & Kathy Lee* and he appeared in an episode of the CBS series *Nash Bridges*. MTV used him on its Celebrity Death Match animated series. He was featured on the cover of *TV Guide* and in a full-length article in *Rolling Stone*.

There was an occasional setback. McMahon had become wild in his hatred for Austin, so he signed the 6' 7", 345-pound behemoth Kane to wrestle Austin in a first-blood match on June 28, 1998. The winner would be the first wrestler to make his opponent bleed. McMahon even convinced Kane to set himself on fire if he failed to win the match. When The Undertaker, who was trying to help Austin, mistakenly leveled Stone Cold with a chair, Kane covered him for the pin to win the title.

The setback lasted only 24 hours. The next night, Austin beat Kane to regain the title and become a two-time WWF World champion.

Austin and The Undertaker reconciled long enough to win the WWF World tag team title from Love and Kane on July 26, 1998, although they lost it two weeks later to the same team. At SummerSlam '98, Austin held off a furious challenge from The Undertaker and retained the belt. After SummerSlam, McMahon intensified his efforts to destroy Austin. He scheduled more three-way matches involving Austin, Kane, and The Undertaker. He revealed that he had a master plan to strip Austin of the title but refused to reveal the details of that plan. "I guarantee you Steve Austin will no longer be WWF World champion after September 27, 1998," McMahon declared.

McMahon was a man of his word. He made Austin wrestle in another three-way match involving Kane and The Undertaker. Austin battled courageously, but the odds were against him. Kane and The Undertaker choke-slammed Stone Cold at the same time before simultaneously pinning him.

McMahon was ecstatic. He ran to the ring and yelled, "Give me the belt!," then ran to his limo and drove away. At the time, nobody knew who the new World champion was. After all, two men can't hold one belt.

McMahon's answer was as devious as his plan to upend Austin. He ordered a match between Kane and The Undertaker and made Austin special referee.

"And if you don't make a three-count and raise one of their hands as champion, I will fire you," McMahon promised.

Austin made a three-count. In fact, he made a pair of three-counts after leveling both Kane and The Undertaker. And he declared a new champion: himself.

McMahon followed through on his promise and fired Austin.

This seemed like the classic case of a man biting off his nose to spite his face. After all, the WWF's surge in popularity was a result of Austin's surge in popularity. McMahon seemed to be killing the golden goose.

Eventually, Shane McMahon, Vince's son, exercised his power as a WWF executive and reinstated Austin. A title tournament was held at the 1998 Survivor Series. Austin beat Big Bossman in the first round, but in the second round he found out that Shane McMahon wasn't really his friend. Shane, the special referee for the match, refused to count Austin's pin of Mankind. McMahon's corporate stooges interfered, and Mankind won the match. Rocky Maivia went on to win the tournament and the WWF World title.

McMahon never stopped scheming, and Austin never stopped fighting. McMahon conspired to make sure he was the last man into the ring for the 1999 Royal Rumble and that Austin was the first. With only Austin and McMahon remaining in the Rumble, Austin knocked out McMahon with a Stone Cold stunner. Austin was ready to eliminate him when Rocky Maivia came out and distracted Austin.

Everyone but the fans seemed to be against Austin in the days before Wrestlemania XIV. As he tried to prepare for his World championship match with Shawn Michaels, scheduled for March 29, 1998, Austin was taunted by Mike Tyson while fellow DeGeneration Xers Michaels and Chyna watched.

This gave McMahon time to sneak up behind Austin and toss him over the top rope for the win.

The match the wrestling world had been waiting for took place on February 14, 1999, at the St. Valentine's Day Massacre pay-per-view: Austin vs. McMahon in a steel cage. McMahon said he had a detailed plan for beating Austin, but his plan apparently wasn't foolproof. Austin brutalized McMahon. He pushed him off the cage and sent him crashing through the broad-caster's table. As medical personnel tried to take McMahon away on a gurney, Austin slammed the stretcher into the cage and pro-ceeded to deliver a brutal beating.

Then, Paul Wight, the wrestler who had been known as The Giant in WCW, cut through the bottom of the cage and charged after Austin. When Wight whipped Austin into the cage, part of the cage fell apart. Austin fell to the floor and was declared the winner. McMahon, had to be carried back to the dressing room.

Of course, the crowd was delighted by all of this. Crowds were delighted by everything Austin did. In 1998, he was voted Wrestler of the Year and Most Popular Wrestler of the Year by the readers of *Pro Wrestling Illustrated* magazine. His popularity showed no signs of abating. But when it ultimately does, as it does to all wrestlers, Steve Austin will know he had a great run, one of the best ever.

"The machine's going to keep moving," he told *Rolling Stone*. "Everyone always gets their feelings hurt when their value starts to go down and they're not the No. 1 guy anymore. Hey, I'm not going to get my feelings hurt. I realize I gotta get it while I can."

Steve Austin is getting it. In 1998, he earned $8 million, quite a raise from $20 a night.

And that's the bottom line.

Chronology

1964   Born Steve Anderson in Austin, Texas, on December 18;
takes stepfather's last name of Williams.

1989   Debuts at the Sportatorium in Dallas and beats Frogman Leblanc.

1990   Voted Rookie of the Year by *Pro Wrestling Illustrated* magazine.

1991   Makes his WCW debut in Houston, Texas, and beats Sam Houston.

Beats Bobby Eaton for the WCW TV title.

1992   Beats Barry Windham for a second WCW TV title.

1993   Teams with Brian Pillman to beat Shane Douglas and Rick Steamboat
for the WCW World tag team title.

Beats Dustin Rhodes at Starrcade for the WCW U.S. title.

1995   Gets fired by WCW, makes his ECW debut, then signs with the WWF.

1996   Wins the WWF King of the Ring Tournament.

1997   Teams with Shawn Michaels to beat Owen Hart and Davey Boy Smith
for his first WWF World tag team title.

Defeats Owen Hart at SummerSlam in East Rutherford, New Jersey,
for his first WWF Intercontinental title.

Defeats Owen Hart at Survivor Series for his second WWF
Intercontinental title.

1998   Wins his first WWF World heavyweight title at WrestleMania XIV
by beating Shawn Michaels.

Wins his second WWF World heavyweight title by beating Kane
in Cleveland, Ohio.

Voted Wrestler of the Year and Most Popular Wrestler of the Year
by *Pro Wrestling Illustrated* magazine.

1999   Takes a break from wrestling at year's end to schedule required neck
surgery, resulting from a piledriver performed on him two years earlier.

Further Reading

Austin, Steve. "The Bottom Line . . . According to Steve Austin."
   Wrestler Digest (Spring 1998): 18–20.

Burkett, Harry. "Austin or McMahon: Who Really Has the
   Upper Hand?" *The Wrestler* (February 1999): 42–45.

Ethier, Bryan. "Even Steven? Why Austin Is Next to Go Corporate."
   The Wrestler (April 1999): 38–41.

Ethier, Bryan. "Stone Cold's Personal Survivor Series."
   Inside Wrestling (January 1999): 34–37.

"Expert Analysis—Austin vs. Goldberg: Who Would Win,
   and Why?" *Inside Wrestling* (November 1998): 34–37.

The official Steve Austin web site can be found at
http://www.stonecold.com

Index

Adams, Chris, 17–19
Adams, Toni, 18, 19
Anderson, Arn, 21, 22, 24, 25
Anderson, Randy, 24
Anderson, Steve, 15
Austin, Steve. *See also* Steve Anderson and Steve Williams
  in ECW, 33, 34
  in Hollywood Blonds, 23–25
  in WCW, 19–33
  WCW TV titles, 21
  WCW U.S. title, 26
  WCW World tag team title, 24
  in WWF, 34–59
  WWF Intercontinental titles, 45, 49
  WWF World heavyweight titles, 13, 53, 57
Badd, Johnny B., 21, 27
Big Bossman, 57
Big Van Vader, 40
Bischoff, Eric, 32–34
Bockwinkel, Nick, 27
Brisco, Jerry, 54
Brown, D-Lo, 49
Brutus Beefcake, 30
Chyna, 12, 52
Clark, Jeannie, 18, 19, 35
Dangerous Alliance, the, 22, 31
Dangerously, Paul E., 22, 23
DeGeneration X, 9, 10, 12, 49, 52, 53

DiBiase, Ted, 34, 37
Douglas, Shane, 23, 24
Dude Love, 54–56
Eaton, Bobby, 21, 22
Edna High School, Austin, Texas, 16
Extreme Championship Wrestling (ECW), 33, 34
Flair, Ric, 31, 37
Giant, the, 58. *See also* Paul Wight
Gorilla Monsoon, 40, 41
Hacksaw Duggan, 27, 29, 30, 31
Hall, Scott, 37
Hart, Bret, 8, 40–44, 53
Hart Foundation, the, 43
Hart, Owen, 7, 43, 44, 49
Hogan, Hulk, 29, 31, 32, 34, 37
Hollywood Blonds, the, 23–25
Hunter Hearst Helmsley, 12, 39, 40, 49, 52, 54, 55
Kane, 55–57
Luger, Lex, 37
Maivia, Rocky, 49, 50, 57
Mankind, 57
McMahon, Shane, 57
McMahon, Vince, Jr., 9, 13, 29, 42, 48–59
Mero, Marc, 38, 39
Michaels, Shawn, 8–13, 40, 41, 43, 44, 51–53
Nash, Kevin, 37
Parker, Colonel Robert, 25, 26
Patterson, Pat, 54
Pillman, Brian, 21, 23–25, 27, 41

Race, Harley, 31
Rhodes, Dustin, 21, 26
Roberts, Jake, 38, 39
Roma, Paul, 24, 25
Ross, Jim, 41
Rude, Rick, 22, 31
Sandman, the, 34
Savage, Randy, 30, 31, 37
Sergeant Slaughter, 48
Shamrock, Ken, 43
Smith, Davey Boy, 43, 44
Steamboat, Ricky, 23, 24, 27
Steiner, Scott, 21
Torg, Dr. Joseph, 47, 48
Turner, Ted, 29, 30
Tyson, Mike, 8–10, 12, 13, 22, 51–53
Undertaker, The, 40, 55–57
United States Wrestling Alliance (USWA), 17, 18
Vega, Savio, 37, 39
Von Erich wrestling family, 16, 17
Whipwreck, Mikey, 34
Wight, Paul, 58, 59
Williams, Steve, 15–17
Windham, Barry, 22
World Championship Wrestling (WCW), 7, 19, 21–25, 27, 29–37, 40, 58, 59
World Wrestling Federation (WWF), 7, 9, 10, 13, 16, 29, 30, 34–48, 50–53
Yokozuna, 39

Photo Credits

All-Star Sports: p. 42; Associated Press/Wide World Photos: pp. 11, 12, 46, 54, 58; Jeff Eisenberg Sports Photography: pp. 2, 8, 14, 17, 28, 30, 36, 38, 48, 51, 60; Sports Action: pp. 6, 20, 33; WCW: pp. 22, 25, 26.

DAN ROSS has spent the past 10 years observing and writing about professional wrestling. His writing on wrestling, basketball, and baseball has appeared in numerous publications around the world, and he is a frequent guest whenever European radio and television stations require an American viewpoint on wrestling. He lives in upstate New York with his wife, son, and dog, and likes to brag to neighbors about the wrestling ring in his basement.